Christmas

Jessica Morrison

Weigl

Published by Weigl Educational Publishers Limited
6325 10th Street SE
Calgary, Alberta
T2H 2Z9

www.weigl.com
Copyright ©2011 Weigl Educational Publishers Limited.
All rights reserved. No part of this publication may be reproduced, stored in a retrieval system, or transmitted in any form or
by any means, electronic, mechanical, photocopying, recording, or otherwise, without the prior written permission
of the publisher.

Library and Archives Canada Cataloguing in Publication data available upon request.
Cataloging-in-Publication Data

ISBN: 978-1-55388-607-5 (hard cover)
ISBN: 978-1-55388-608-2 (soft cover)

Printed in the United States of America in North Mankato, Minnesota
1 2 3 4 5 6 7 8 9 0 14 13 12 11 10

062010
WEP230610

Editor: Josh Skapin
Design: Terry Paulhus

Every reasonable effort has been made to trace ownership and to obtain permission to reprint copyright material.
The publishers would be pleased to have any errors or omissions brought to their attention so that they may be
corrected in subsequent printings.

Weigl acknowledges Getty Images as its primary image supplier for this title.

We gratefully acknowledge the financial support of the Government of Canada through the Canada Book Fund for our
publishing activities.

Contents

What is Christmas Day?

Christmas Day is on December 25. Many people celebrate the birth of Jesus Christ on this day. Christians believe Jesus is the son of God. The story of Jesus' birth is told in the Bible. Christmas is the most widely celebrated holiday in Canada.

Christmas History

It is believed that Jesus was born about 2,000 years ago. However, no one knows the exact date of his birth. In the fourth century, Christians chose December 25 to celebrate the Feast of the **Nativity**. Today, families still gather for a special meal and to give gifts. Gifts are wrapped in colourful paper and placed under the Christmas tree. They are opened on Christmas Eve or Christmas Day.

Canada's First Christmas

One of the first known Christmas celebrations in Canada was in 1535. French explorer Jacques Cartier was on his second trip to Canada. He was in search of riches to bring home to France. Cartier and his crew had a small Christmas feast in Canada. They had little food to spare. The meal was made up of spoiled vegetables and salted meat.

Symbols of Christmas

Many people put up a Christmas tree. They decorate an **evergreen** tree with glass bulbs and ribbons. Canadians often decorate the outside of their home. They put up coloured lights. Some people have a small crèche. A crèche is a model of the stable where Christ was born.

Celebrating Across Canada

There are many cultures living in Canada. Each has it own Christmas traditions. Many Scandinavian Canadians start the Christmas season on December 13. This is St. Lucia Day. St. Lucia is a symbol of light. A family's oldest daughter dresses up as St. Lucia. She wears a crown of candles and a white dress with a red sash. She brings her family fresh saffron buns.

A Ukrainian Christmas

Ukrainians celebrate Christmas Day on January 7. Events begin when the first star is sighted on Christmas Eve. The father of the house gives a blessing. Then, he places a sheaf of wheat in the house. The wheat is a symbol of the family gathering. A large, meatless meal is served. Hay is placed under the table and tablecloth. It represents Jesus' manger.

Special Visitors

Many children look forward to a visit from Santa Claus. Santa leaves presents for children on Christmas Eve. He travels from house to house in a sleigh pulled by flying reindeer. Santa wears a red suit and has a white beard. In Newfoundland, another type of visitor comes to people's houses. Mummers are people who wear masks and costumes. They entertain their hosts for baked goods and other sweets.

Parades, Pageants, and Parties

Christmas celebrations often start in early December. Some families attend pageants. These are plays about the birth of Jesus Christ. Many people attend Christmas parties. These parties may include a special meal, singing, or treats. Christmas parades take place in many towns and cities. **Floats** are driven down streets, and bands play music during parades.

Christmas Eve

Some people begin their Christmas celebrations on Christmas Eve. This is the night before Christmas Day. Many families attend a midnight church service. In Quebec, some families return home to eat a huge meal. The meal is called *réveillon*. A *tourtière*, or meat pie, is often served.

Sounds of Christmas

Carols are songs about Christmas. They are joyful songs about different aspects of the Christmas season. Sometimes, carollers go door-to-door to sing carols. Well-known Christmas carols include *Jingle Bells* and *Rudolph the Red-nosed Reindeer.* Canada's first Christmas carol was written in the early 1600s. Father Jean de Brébeuf wrote *The Huron Carol* to help explain the story of the birth of Jesus to Aboriginal Peoples.

The Huron Carol

'Twas in the moon of wintertime
When all the birds had fled
That mighty Gitchi Manitou
Sent angel choirs instead
Before their light the stars grew dim
And wandering hunters heard the hymn:
"Jesus your King is born
Jesus is born: in excelsis gloria!"

Within a lodge of broken bark
The tender babe was found,
A ragged robe of rabbit skin
Enwrapped his beauty 'round
And as the hunter braves drew nigh
The angel song rang loud and high:
"Jesus your King is born
Jesus is born: in excelsis gloria!"

The earliest moon of wintertime
Is not so round and fair
As was the ring of glory on
The helpless infant there
The chiefs from far before him knelt
With gifts of fox and beaver pelt
"Jesus your King is born,
Jesus is born: in excelsis gloria!"

O children of the forest free
O sons of Manitou,
The holy child of earth and heaven
Is born today for you.
Come kneel before the radiant boy
Who brings you beauty, peace, and joy
"Jesus your King is born,
Jesus is born: in excelsis gloria!"

23

Glossary

Index

carols	evergreen
floats	nativity